Anonymous

The Starling of the Spire

A Bird's View of the Church as it was

Anonymous

The Starling of the Spire
A Bird's View of the Church as it was

ISBN/EAN: 9783337004200

Printed in Europe, USA, Canada, Australia, Japan

Cover: Foto ©ninafisch / pixelio.de

More available books at **www.hansebooks.com**

The Starling of the Spire.

—◆—

"A bird of the air shall carry the voice, and that which
hath wings shall tell the matter."

Eccles. **x, 20.**

I'm a starling endow'd with wondrous sense,
   Which is rare in these modern days ; ·
And presume to chatter, with some pretence,
   Of my knowledge of Parsons' ways.

All my early life was joyously spent,
   In and near a most noble church ;
I knew ev'ry stone of its battlement,
   And each crocket I made my perch.

Very high was the spire, its structure light ;
   And architects often have said,
That but few in this land surpass'd its height,
   Their remarks enlighten'd my head.

They've agreed that the flying buttress too,
    In our country was seldom seen;
With such men as these, I've had much to do,
    For amongst them I've often been.

As the stranger has view'd the eastern end,
    I've listen'd to what he would say;
And have notic'd that one, much time would spend,
    Whilst another would walk away.

Both the cross and crown of thorns, form'd the gem
    Of this architectural sight;
And the graceful form of the diadem,
    Stood out well in the mellow'd light.

I have quaked at times when the thunder's crash
    Has awoke me at night from sleep;
And still more have I fear'd the lightning's flash,
    Might lay all in a crumbling heap.

Very proudly I've watch'd the stately spire,
    When the play of the storm was spent;
Rejoic'd that no shocks of electric fire,
    The time-honour'd fabric had rent.

'Neath its shade hard by did the Rect'ry stand,
  Surrounded by many a tree;
As we Starlings (of course) had full command,
  We were happy as birds could be.

Whilst sitting one day in a musing mood,
  The bells chiming sweetly and clear,
'Twas a fancy of mine, the peal was good,
  And their melody charm'd my ear.

They merrily rang a new Bishop in,
  Which made me most eager to know,
How amongst his flock he meant to begin,
  So I flew about to and fro!

To the Rector's house in the ev'ning came,
  Some neighbouring Parsons to dine;
As I soon discover'd this Prelate's aim,
  Was to meet his Clergy (in fine.)

Into rooms I peep'd with curious eyes,
  And listen'd at every nook;
His lordship, I fancied, was very wise,
  As a charm attended his look.

How cautious all were, how mild and how good!
Each sought an impression to make:
Most thoughtfully too they partook of food,
Whilst none *too* much wine dar'd to take.

The Curates look'd meek; but, I knew not why,
The Rectors and Vicars more free:
But to *all*, it matter'd not who were nigh,
The Bishop was kind as could be.

They had much to discuss from far and near,
Oh! their hearts with such zeal were fill'd!
And as *he* attracted each Parson's ear,
Some godly advice was instill'd.

I observ'd that these were a favor'd few,
Allow'd a more fortunate chance;
(In the morning their numbers largely grew,
As to Church I saw them advance.)

But just as I left, for my nightly perch,
I flew round the rooms once again;
What pleas'd me the most in my eager search,
Oh listen! all Clerical men.

By the light of a lamp that Bishop read,
With a countenance all benign;
On the Holy Bible the beams were shed,
For he treasur'd each sacred line.

He glean'd from its pages his solemn trust,
Then devoutly he bent the knee;
To be faithful to God he felt he must
In prayer for his help often be.

I moraliz'd long at that silent hour,
Being wrapt in a pensive mood:
I said to myself, " *Now*, I've learn'd the power,
And the secret of doing good!"

It struck me, perchance, I could seek the homes,
Of some neighbouring Parish Priests;
For 'tis nothing strange, if a Starling roams,
Over country, or towns and streets.

So off to the belfry I flew away,
To dream o'er my evening's sight;
Determin'd to stay in the Church next day,
And be there with the dawning light.

* * * * * * *

The bells rang again on the morrow's morn,
    And I sought out a snug retreat;
To quiz not, I vow, for *that* I should scorn,
    So demurely I took my seat.

In a darken'd corner, unseen by all,
    With cobwebs in plenty for shade;
I look'd on the choir, the nave, and the stall,
    And my patience was well repaid.

As the Clergy pass'd by in robes of black,
    With the Prelate in one of white,
Why surely of Priests there can be no lack,
    I thought: but alas! 'twas not right.

They were seated at last, and then a charge
    The Bishop deliver'd to all:
Oh *who* could behold that number so large,
    And not solemn feelings recall?

He told them that need there was now for prayer,
    He spake of the thousands who die,
With no one to seek them, no one to care,
    For the outcast's penitent cry.

He spake of the homes and the dens of vice,
    Where their presence might comfort bring,
And by Christian acts of love entice,
    Till sorrow each bosom should wring.

Of the lonely widow and cottage poor,
    And the heart-broken orphan child,
Where no Minister comes to seek their door,
    And console them with accents mild.

He drew a dark picture of foreign lands,
    Where they never had heard of God;
Of the heathen untaught on Afric's sands,
    And the scourge of the Slaver's rod!

He enlarg'd on the need of faithful men,
    In those districts remote and vast,
Of money for building Churches, and then
    What glory on England might last.

He urg'd on them always to dwell in love,
    To fulfil the Divine commands:
To rest all their hopes on a home above,
    And to strengthen each other's hands.

B

He warn'd them of error, in language kind,
(For the tempter was ever near),
He told them to cherish an humble mind,
Nor forget they were pilgrims here.

Their flocks were in danger, in days like these,
If shepherds deserted their post;
How could they contentedly dwell at ease,
Whilst Satan was busy the most!

Here he paus'd—and gently a sigh escap'd,
Follow'd closely by vows and prayers,
From many; though others too often gap'd,
All engross'd by their worldly cares.

Then follow'd the blessing, and each arose,
While their names were call'd out aloud,
They answer'd if there, as ev'ry one knows;
When 'twas over—the Proctor bow'd.

Thus ended the scene, and the Church was hus]
In its stillness and death-like gloom:
I waited no longer; but quickly rush'd
To my friends in the belfry room.

And now for a time I remain'd at home,
　With my future plans to arrange;
In the coming winter I fix'd to roam,
　And indulge in this hobby strange.

I thought that a convocation of birds
　Might assist me by their advice;
But their constant chatter and flow of words,
　Would not be, perhaps, very nice.

And then if they quarrell'd, how very wrong,
　For birds, like mankind, can't agree,
Unless they're endow'd with a wisdom strong,
　And a spirit of charity!

So all things consider'd, my secret slept,
　And my council was never call'd.
'Tis comfort to know that one's mind is kept,
　From the sense of being enthrall'd!

*　　*　　*　　*　　*　　*　　*

The fogs of the autumn had roll'd away,
　For long had they shrouded the spire;
A sunshiny, bracing, and frosty day,
　Was a change we must all admire.

I quitted the town for a country life,
    Rejoicing in ambient air;
Nothing loth to escape its noise and strife,
    To commence my inspection there.

A lovely village attracted my gaze,
    As the sun was about to set,
Such a fairy land it look'd in the haze,
    That my mind reverts to it yet.

The Church was embosom'd in lofty trees,
    And ivy crept over its tow'r;
Close shelter'd, from every chilling breeze,
    Round its walls grew many a flow'r.

The fading beams, with their deepening hue,
    Seem'd to flit o'er the sculptured cross,
And hanging willow, with darkening yew,
    Told the tale of the heart's deep loss.

In a rookery near I sought a nest,
    Where the oak and the wytch elm grew;
It suited my wings to enjoy some rest,
    As the ground was cover'd with dew.

The beautiful woodland ascended high
  Near a lake in the distant vale ;
Fair nature had blended her sweets to try
  And give pleasure within this dale.

The mansion was large, in the Gothic style,
  Like an old baronial hall ;
An ancient grandeur embellish'd the pile,
  And heraldry blaz'd on its wall.

Its owner for years had in orders been,
  (As a family living pass'd
From father to son, or the next of kin,
  Like an heir-loom ever to last.)

It puzzled me often, I must confess,
  When I saw him throughout the week
In hunting costume ; and in change of dress,
  He would sometimes profanely speak.

Much care was bestow'd on his handsome stud,
  For his stables were quite his pride ;
I've watch'd him return all cover'd with mud,
  After many a hard day's ride.

His duties were many, and well fulfill'd,
  On the bench or at weekly board;
In politics too he was also skill'd,
  And with knowledge his head was stor'd.

I fear that his own ordination vows
  Too seldom return'd to his mind,
'Tis sad when the judgment to pleasure bows,
  Leaving conscience asleep behind.

His son was his Curate, and did his best
  To resemble his worthy sire;
Their sports they pursued with far greater zest
  Than what holier aims inspire.

There was one of his daughters, fair and good
  (A Starling can judge but by ways);
In all parish visits she foremost stood:
  'Tis but right I award her praise.

I have seldom look'd on a face so sweet
  As that of the beautiful Maude,
For often unwittingly we did meet,
  On her errands of love abroad.

Her footfall I've heard on the crispy grass,
　As quickly and lightly she went;
It always rejoic'd me to watch her pass,
　On her mission of kindness bent.

She had found no charm in the world's gay sphere,
　Though its brightest forms she had seen;
They but help'd to entrance the soul whilst here,
　And from heavenly objects wean.

Not a fitful zeal did her heart possess,
　Nor in vain had baptismal vows
Been uttered, meaningless things to express,
　As the worldling often allows.

I was just deciding to end my stay,
　When a whisper breath'd through the park,
From voices familiar, grave, and gay,
　Of which I had been in the dark.

I flew unperceiv'd to the servants' hall
　One night, and relinquish'd my sleep;
Most slyly I settled outside its wall—
　For Starlings you know are so deep.

Miss Maude had collected her father's poor,
    To bid them a parting adieu,
And as presents for each adorn'd the floor,
    The tears that were shed were not few.

" She was just what a Parson's wife should be,"
    They said, " but her loss they would feel."
The bells in the morning told merrily
    Her bridal for woe or for weal.

I care not to witness events like these,
    Being common with birds and men;
But when they occur amongst the grandees,
    They are far more attractive then.

And a special fancy allur'd me on
    To a lancet window I knew;
Such a fair young bride as we look'd upon
    Had drawn all the neighbourhood too.

As the sun in its brightest glory shone
    On her bridal and chaste attire,
It betokened blessings on her from one
    Whose love was her truest desire.

All vanish'd—and scenes of a festive kind
  Whil'd away the remaining hours;
Both nature and art in beauty combin'd,
  And *recherchés* were fruit and flowers.

'Twas a brilliant sight, when the hall was lit,
  And the table display'd its plate,
To see lords and ladies together sit
  At the Rector's in costly state.

Both Fortnum and Gunter prestige maintain'd
  In the sumptuous bill of fare;
Whist settled the old as the ev'ning waned,
  Terpsichore, youth and the fair.

I peer'd through the curtains,—then took my leave,
  Amaz'd at such glitter and show:
I thought it was scarcely the kind of eve
  For apostles of Christ below.

*   *   *   *   *   *   *

There were certain times when the Clergy met,
  To partake of the bounteous cheer
At the Rector's hall, when covers were set
  For his brethren from far and near.

All sorts then assembled—the high and low,
 And broad, or what name you may please;
The Rector of course would politeness shew
 To Oxford Divines, or St. Bees'.

But *one* poor Curate was always a guest,
 And excited my feelings sore;
In a coat, alas! not one of the best,
 He appear'd at his Rector's door.

Transferr'd it had been by charity's hand
 From the pluralist's well-clothed back,
Whose servants behind him would daily stand,
 In gorgeous array without lack.

After such a *réunion* I was led
 To discover this Curate's home;
As he walk'd, I watch'd the way he would tread,
 It was dreary and wearisome.

He had scarcely quitted the warm saloon,
 Ere a snow storm thicken'd the air:
But he brav'd the cold, and the mantled moon
 Help'd him onward his toil to bear.

I saw him enter his humble abode—
   It was long past the dead of night;
His industrious wife for hours had sew'd
   By one dismal dull candle's light.

Nothing strange it seem'd, for her eyes were dim,
   (A crevice disclos'd her employ)
But how thankfully did she welcome him,
   Most fondly expressing her joy.

It was pinching work, with a stipend small,
   (Not more than a hundred a year)
To satisfy each necessitous call,
   When provisions were very dear.

And I heard as a fact 'twas all they had,
   (With eight little children to feed)
But it tried them most when a case more sad
   Came before them of bitter need.

The mite they bestow'd with a loving heart
   Cost them self-denial unknown;
From family comforts they'd sooner part,
   Than refuse a poor starving one!

Their household by method was ruled aright,
  · And leisure for teaching secur'd;
They aided parochial schools in spite
  Of numerous hardships endur'd.

A faithful domestic, whose orphan life
  Had been nurtur'd beneath their roof,
Was the only help of the Curate's wife,
  Though poverty tested her worth.

I witness'd a Christmas festival there;
  On its joyous and merry eve
Both parents and children forgot their care,
  In the garlands I saw them weave.

With laurel and holly their room was drest,
  Each wishing to add a fresh bough;
The children all pleas'd were cloth'd in their best—
  A thing they could seldom allow.

The yule log look'd bright, and tea was prepar'd;
  · A cake at this season was made,
For some poor parishioners always shar'd
  The frugal repast that they laid.

They sang Christmas carols in concert sweet,
  Infant voices together rose;
It look'd *well* the Pastor his flock should meet,
  And with praises the ev'ning close.

No feature of interest mark'd the church,
  Or bespoke any outward grace,
Not even the cypress or silver birch,
  Screening neatly the sacred place.

Its discordant bell, although crack'd and old,
  On the great Nativity's morn
Assembled a group I lik'd to behold,
  To hear of their Lord being born.

An earnest discourse full of Gospel truths,
  That the weakest mind could receive,
Told of peace and good will to all who'd choose
  Their Saviour in faith to believe.

He caution'd communicants, ere they came
  To His Table, to prove their hearts,
That their lives be holy and free from blame,
  Shewing fruits the Spirit imparts.

It happen'd I heard what the people thought
   Of this plain unpretending Priest,
From the Sexton's lips, and I knew he ought
   To be judge of his *ways* at least.

As he slowly dug on, he gravely said
   To a list'ning dissenting friend:
" The man who lies now in his coffin dead,
   Has been spared a most awful end!

" A greater infidel never did walk,
   'Or such harm in the place had done;
'Twas shocking to hear his blasphemous talk—
   No worse could be under the sun.

" But thanks to his Minister, under God,
   The Bible was true, he confess'd,
And now with comfort I turn up this sod,
   With hope that he's gone to his rest.

" They needn't have Chapels, if men like ours
   Stood up in the Churches to preach;
And pity it is that, with all his pow'rs,
   He has not more people to teach.

" When any are ill or dying, he goes
  To pray by their beds or console;
To Churchmen alike with Methodists, shews
  How he values a precious soul!"

*　　*　　*　　*　　*　　*　　*

Spring flowers were peeping from under leaves,
  With charming profusion and scent,
And sparrows were chirping on cottage eaves,
  As flying above them I went.

I chanc'd to observe a cross on a pump,
  That stood in a garden hard by
The place where I stopp'd, on an old tree stump,
  And ponder'd awhile to know why.

My curious mind discover'd the fact,
  'Twas the Vicar's pump I had found;
Offence it had giv'n, being judg'd an act
  Too Popish for Protestant ground.

Too far he'd exceeded the Church's use
  In symbols and crosses and albs;
And some had been heard this Priest to accuse
  Of int'rest in Romish cabals.

Whatever he was, a celibate life
  Was right in *his* office, he said :
The parish lost much, as a useful wife
  Might his judgment have rightly led.

In our Anglican Church, his vestments strange
  Bewilder'd the ignorant poor ;
Innovations like these produced a change,
  And drove them to Meeting-house door.

The eight o'clock bell chim'd for him alone,
  For his household, (a scanty few)
Had stoutly refus'd their prayers to intone,
  Professing they'd too much to do.

Great things were expected when Easter came,
  So the villagers all declared,
Profuse decorations appear'd his aim
  In his Church, and no pains were spared.

The altar seem'd far the most sacred spot,
  With its candles and crucifix ;
And choicest exotics that could be got
  Adorn'd the gold Chalice and Pix.

The pure simple service of Easter Day
  Was veil'd in mysterious forms;
Genuflexions and rites help'd not t' allay
  The sinner whose conscience had qualms.

The Priest did not kneel for the Spirit's aid,
  Ere in surplice he rose to preach;
I knew not why such omission was made—
  Like his words, 'twas beyond my reach.

Not even the Holy Eucharist drew
  Willing steps from a number great,
As I saw when over how very few
  Left the Church, through the Churchyard gate.

It was on this noted "Lord's day of joy,"
  The font for immersion receiv'd
A mother's pale, delicate baby-boy,
  " More water—more grace" she believ'd!

It shiver'd when plac'd in its mother's arms,
  She fear'd any longer to stay;
Convulsions occasion'd the worst alarms,
  And slowly its life ebb'd away.

D

A hubbub succeeded—the people vow'd
  Their infants should go unbaptiz'd,
If customs uncheck'd should be still allow'd,
  And opinions were undisguis'd.

The Vicar had fail'd thus to win their love
  By his formal and rigid code;
The Saints he'd extoll'd more than Christ above,
  And lauded the " Mother of God."

It suited his Sabbatarian views,
  To keep strictly the service hours;
After which by train he often would choose
  To recruit his bodily pow'rs.

The village was left to dissent or games,
  On its winter and summer eve,
And Chapels abounded with pressing claims,
  Trying moral good to achieve.

What with hockey and quoits, God's holy law
  Was profan'd on His blessed day:
Such scenes discourag'd my reverent awe
  And I could not in conscience stay!

*   *   *   *   *   *   *

Two persons were once most deeply engross'd
  Near a Church I much wish'd to see;
Re-building the Chancel was uppermost,
  And they did not at all agree.

The Squire and Incumbent, I soon inferr'd,
  Had different plans of their own,
And sadly a spirit of discord stirr'd
  What had better been left alone.

The latter, for popularity's sake,
  (Seeking Nonconformist applause)
Would hardly a Churchman's opinions take,
  Or treated them lightly as straws.

The former, whose acres enrich'd his purse,
  As Lay-Rector receiv'd the tithes,
But to low Church ways was ever averse,
  Hence the quarrels that would arise.

He contended the good old times were best,
  When repairs were done by a rate;
And these days of reform he hated, lest
  The Church be divided from state.

His mind he spoke freely, as proud blood flow'd
 Through his aristocratic veins:
" Mr. Vicar, you've too great leaning shew'd
 To dissent—your Bishop complains.

" You undermine Sacraments Christ ordain'd,
 By your heterodoxical views;
Dissenter in heart, you are still maintain'd
 By a cure you like not to lose.

" Times are changed since the Parson used to dine
 In silk stockings and buckles bright,
And could drink his bottle or two of wine,
 With a rubber of whist at night.

" At any mix'd meeting you take the chair,
 Forgetting your office and gown,
And you meet all sorts of Ministers there!
 Do you do it to gain renown?

" Too seldom at home, too often abroad,
 Believe me I hear of your ways;
You aim not so much to glorify God,
 As you seek to court human praise.

" When you're smoking your pipe (a habit bad)
  With your friends at the midnight hour,
It seems to my mind deplorably sad
  To resist not temptation's pow'r.

" You check not the spirit of parish news
  By a dignified, quiet air;
But gladly the village tea-table choose,
  Where its scandal is welcom'd there.

" And now you oppose restoring God's House,
  Befitting his temple and shrine,
Because your allies, with whom you carouse,
  Against decorations combine."

I eagerly caught up the Vicar's words,
  As he answer'd the charges grave:
Who can fathom the minds of clever birds,
  Or explain the instinct they have?

" ' Facts are stubborn things,' though times, Sir,
      are bad,
  I think I can prove they were worse
Ere villages resident Clergy had,
  A step to which most were averse.

" In cheerful towns they selected abodes,
  Far off from their several cures,
When often excuses of dreadful roads
  Deterr'd them from fens and from moors.

" A winter's neglect reach'd a Bishop's ears,
  Who reprovéd the Parish Priest,
But he tried to assuage his Lordship's fears,
  Not abash'd in the very least.

" ' No parson could travel by such a way,
  I'm assur'd,' he coolly replied,
And I'll shepherd my flock the first spring day,
  When it's fit for myself to ride.

" What think you when one also stacked his hay
  Within the Church Porch to keep dry, ʃ
And until his pony eat it away,
  He never for service came nigh?

" Another relinquish'd his pulpit once
  For a time, to a sitting goose,
As there she fancied herself to ensconce,
  Till she found she could spare its use.

" Do'nt be shock'd to hear that one bought a pig
  After prayers on a sabbath morn,
In a sack he took it home in his gig,
  To eat up the refuse of corn.

" A Priest, whom I knew, liked his port too well,
  And his clerk used to lead him·home ;
But many delinquencies could I tell,
  You've obliged me to give you some.

" An Oxford Divine, a long time ago,
  Who drove ev'ry Sunday some miles,
His fighting cocks kept in his pulpit low,
  Tied up in a basket meanwhiles.

" It suited him well, for the Monday's fight
  Came off not much further that way,
It troubled him little (with conscience light)
  So long as the birds quiet lay.

" I've heard of an Irish Bishop, who took
  Such pleasure in fishing, that he
In driving to Church, was tempted to hook
  A Salmon he happen'd to see.

" It pains me to state such cases as these,
    'Tis only the contrast to shew
How Parsons themselves seem'd only to please,
    But now they have plenty to do.

" Can you wonder dissent was rampant then,
    So short of our duties we came,
When ungodly and inconsistent men
    Were ordain'd for mere worldly aim?

" By mixing amongst parishioners more,
    And exerting an influence right,
I can truly say I visit their door
    To spend a few hours at night.

" When I see they dislike our rites and forms,
    As the poor nearly always do,
If I can, I steer clear of parish storms,
    My conviction approves it too.

" You must own my congregations increase,
    It is wiser to draw than drive;
By driving, schismatics will not decrease,
    Then to win them back I will strive!"

I left them to settle as best they could,
　　How it ended I never knew,
It seem'd as if neither did any good,
　　So away from the scene I flew.

＊　　＊　　＊　　＊　　＊　　＊　　＊

I settled ere long in a village small,
　　Where neatness and order prevail'd;
And, judging by cottages one and all,
　　The appearance of want was veil'd.

The Parson with scrupulous taste and care
　　Had demolish'd each pauper's hut;
Having means in plenty and much to spare,
　　He'd banish'd the slattern and slut.

The villagers knew not why tidy clothes,
　　When hanging on hedges to dry,
Could give such offence, and quarrels arose
　　When blaming his critical eye.

He was not beloved, for o'erweening pride
　　Peep'd out notwithstanding his gown;
And often his neighbours would pass aside
　　Than stay to encounter his frown.

E

It kept him from many an act of love,
  Repelling the sympathy kind;
The poor could but seldom his feelings move,
  Or attract his ambitious mind.

Once the Clerk and village Master dared
  To express their thoughts near my ears:
" It was only the great for whom he cared,
  Oh how paltry such pride appears!

" No family honours of any date
  Could he claim for himself, not he!
But *they* always assume a pompous gait,
  Who would bigger than others be.

" Did the Clergy but see what pow'r they lose
  When yielding their duties to ease,
To do right, one would think, they'd rather choose,
  Preferring their Master to please."

  * * * * * * *

The warm summer months with my mate I spent,
  In a very retired hole
Of a fine old tree, that the wind had rent,
  And left us our nest in its bole.

We mourn'd over one of our little brood,
    As five birds were reduced to four,
It fell to my lot to provide them food,
    And no fledglings could well eat more.

I regain'd my freedom when harvest came,
    (For our Starlings had ceas'd to tease)
Being tired of leading a life so tame,
    I long'd for the stubbles and trees.

On the back of a sheep I've sometimes sat,
    Watching gleaners with busy hands;
Amus'd with their gossiping, friendly chat,
    As they've wander'd about in bands.

I gather'd up fragments of parish praise,
    Which enrich'd my increasing store—
Their Parson seem'd always contriving ways
    To gladden the hearts of the poor.

He'd ask'd them most kindly to render thanks
    For a bounteous harvest year;
To meet in God's house, where men of all ranks
    Would assemble for worship there.

His night schools they spoke of as public boon,
  With the books they much loved to read,
And trusted he would re-open them soon,
  For they help'd them to learn indeed.

Such a glowing report induced my mind
  To judge for myself of its truth;
So leaving my family cares behind,
  I took to my rambles, forsooth.

I shortly repair'd to the neighb'ring town,
  The sphere of these labours of love;
Dead leaves of autumn were pattering down,
  The sky was all murky above.

A glimmering light from his study fire
  Shed its beam on the Pastor's face,
As he enter'd wet and bedaub'd with mire,
  From a sick and distressing case.

The good man's lamp lighted many an eye,
  'Twas in truth a tell-tale to me;
How little he knew a tattler was nigh,
  Or that one from without could see!

It shone on the young disciples, who sought
    Their endear'd Catechiser's aid;
He strove most earnestly they should be taught,
    And with each one fervently pray'd.

To explain the Eucharist's solemn rite,
    Its use and (too often) abuse,
A lecture each month he would give at night,
    That none might his conscience excuse.

With Bible and Prayer-book beneath his arm,
    To any lone garret he went,
No fever infectious—no fear of harm
    Deterr'd him from where he was bent.

I noticed each Saturday's eve he pass'd
    With his Curates in solemn prayer,
Seeking strength to fulfil their work so vast,
    And their burdens together bear.

They implor'd a blessing on Sabbath hours,
    That their preaching be not in vain,
But devoting to God their souls' best pow'rs,
    The word might " distil as the rain."

By the numbers at Church who throng'd to hear,
   It return'd not to heaven void;
Their warnings check'd many a scoffing jeer,
   In contrast with joys unalloy'd.

*   *   *   *   *   *   *

I'm asham'd to admit, I've peep'd sometimes
   Into vestry windows in towns,
When service began, as I knew by chimes,
   To see Parsons put on their gowns.

Some would carefully re-arrange their hair
   With admiring looks in the glass,
Smoothing down their bands with the nicest care,
   To produce an effect—alas!

And anxious to take a pleasing *coup-d'œil*
   Of their cassock and stole and hood,
Would eagerly gaze for a little while,
   Looking round to see all they could.

But others seem'd never to seek the glass
   As they stood for the Clerk to attire,
They have knelt instead on the well-worn bass,
   With their minds set on things far higher.

In many a village, many a town,
   I've found faithful, devoted men,
Adorning the Church, I most freely own,
   And whose worth I willingly pen.

Of such was the Pastor, whose well-earn'd praise
   Winds up all that I have to tell:
I hope you'll look kindly on Starlings' lays:
   And now I will bid you farewell!

THE END.

Jacksons and Co., Printers, Market-place, Louth.

www.ingramcontent.com/pod-product-compliance
Lightning Source LLC
Chambersburg PA
CBHW021451090426

42739CB00009B/1720